MY BEST JOËL ROBUCHON

ALAIN DUCASSE
PUBLISHING

JOËL ROBUCHON

I opened Restaurant Joël Robuchon. In 1990 I was crowned Chef of the Century and Restaurant Joël Robuchon was named the Best Restaurant in the World by the *International Herald Tribune*. In July 1996, at the age of fifty-one, I retired from cooking in my Paris restaurants to devote my efforts to passing on my expertise and skills. I'm also making the most of my time to do the things that were off-limits to me before: travel, observe, and draw on the knowledge and techniques of other cuisines. Since 1996, through the television shows *Cuisinez comme un grand chef* and later *Bon appétit bien sûr*, produced together with my friend Guy Job, I was able to broadcast the expertise and tricks of leading chefs to food-loving viewers.

Your Compagnon (guild) name is Poitevin la Fidélité. What is the reason for this?

I was born in Poitiers on July 7, 1945. My father was a mason and my mother was a cleaning woman. At the age of twelve, I entered the junior seminary in Mauléon-sur-Sèvre. I discovered my passion for cooking through my contact with the nuns in the seminary kitchen. In 1960 I became an apprentice chef at the Relais de Poitiers hotel, where for three years I learned all the basic culinary techniques. At the age of twenty-one I became a Compagnon du Tour de France des Devoirs Unis (French organization of craftsmen and artisans, a successor to the medieval guild system). This experience was doubly decisive for my incipient career: I trained with chefs from all over France and I was able to strengthen my moral, manual, and physical values.

So young and already a chef?

In 1974, at the age of twenty-eight, I was already at the head ôf a brigade of eighty cooks at the Hôtel Concorde-Lafayette, which served three thousand covers every day. In 1976 I was awarded the title of Meilleur Ouvrier de France (Best Artisan in France), a competition I would later preside over between 1991 and 2005. In 1981 I opened my first restaurant in the 16th arrondissement, Jamin, which in three years was awarded three successive Michelin stars. In late 1993 I moved into a premises in Avenue Raymond-Poincaré, where

Then you created a new concept: the Atelier?

In 2002 I opened a restaurant with a completely innovative concept, a more casual establishment that was more accessible and especially more in keeping with the expectations of our clientèle. I was inspired by Japanese sushi bars and Spanish tapas bars. I designed the project with the renowned architect Pierre-Yves Rochon, who created a dining space that was totally open to the kitchen, and where the comfort of patrons was studied and enhanced to the maximum. In May 2003, l'Atelier de Joël Robuchon opened in Paris and Tokyo, and aroused great interest in the French and international press. With this new concept, I wanted customers to be able to see the products and observe their preparation. For me, the Ateliers are like theaters, where the customers are the audience. Something is always happening; there's always something to see. The hardest thing about cooking is keeping it simple. When it's simple, if it's going to be good, it has to be done well.

After Paris, Monaco?

In 2004 I opened an establishment at the Hôtel Métropole in Monaco. We offer contemporary cuisine there. And there, as with the Ateliers, the kitchen is open to the dining area. As I had always been interested in Japanese cuisine, I opened my first Japanese restaurant, Yoshi, in 2008 inside the same hotel, and its formula was elegance, precision, and warmth.

1966	1976
Became Compagnon du Tour de France des Devoirs Unis	Named Meilleur Ouvrier de France (Best Artisan in France)

Why Japan?

Japanese culture has always been a passion of mine. In 1989 I exported French refinement to my Château Restaurant located in the heart of Tokyo.

Then came China, followed by the United States?

In 2001 I opened at the Lisboa Hotel in Macau, then in 2012 I opened the Robuchon au Dôme fine-dining restaurant inside the Grand Lisboa Hotel. In 2005 the famous MGM Grand Hotel gave me the opportunity to make my American dream come true by asking me to open two restaurants: an Atelier and a fine-dining restaurant. The CEO of MGM Grand, who has fine gourmet taste, gave me carte blanche to create a fine-dining restaurant on a more human scale—with about forty covers— next to the Atelier, which was awarded three Michelin stars.

London, then Hong Kong?

I opened an Atelier de Joël Robuchon in London in 2006, spanning three floors of a building in the Covent Garden theater district. Hong Kong was where I opened my sixth Atelier, with a menu adapted to local produce and customs. I've always wanted to give preference to local produce, which is much better than imported produce. In October 2009, I opened new Ateliers in Taipei. Étoile, in Paris, an Atelier and a fine-dining restaurant in Singapore. I had a busy year in 2015. I opened an Atelier in Bangkok and a fine-dining restaurant in Bordeaux inside my friend Bernard Magrez's hotel, La Grande Maison. I'll be opening Ateliers in Shanghai, New York, Montreal, Geneva, and Miami.

What is your goal?

Passing on things has always been essential for me. Thanks to my many establishments, in France and elsewhere, I have been able to train a large number of chefs of all nationalities and instill in them my belief in the search for excellence and discipline. These chefs today are formidable ambassadors of French cuisine. As a Compagnon, I've learned one thing: Even if you think you've done something well, it can always be done better. And there is no greater personal satisfaction than giving the best of yourself.

GOURMET **PORTRAIT**

1/WHAT IS THE UTENSIL OR INGREDIENT YOU CAN'T COOK WITHOUT?
A small carving fork and, naturally, the potato.

2/WHAT IS YOUR FAVORITE DRINK?
Champagne.

3/WHAT IS THE COOKBOOK THAT MOST INFLUENCED YOU?
L'Heptaméron des Gourmets ou les Délices de la Cuisine Française by Édouard Nignon.

4/WHAT ARE YOUR SECRET WEAKNESSES?
Caviar and truffles.

5/IF YOU HADN'T BEEN A CHEF, WHAT WOULD YOU HAVE LIKED TO BECOME?
An architect.

6/WHAT DO YOU COLLECT?
Connected objects.

7/WHAT IS YOUR MOTTO?
To double your happiness, you have to share it.

1984
|
Obtained three Michelin stars at Jamin in Paris

1990
|
Restaurant Joël Robuchon named Best Restaurant in the World by the International Herald Tribune

1994
|
Named Chef of the Century by the Gault & Millau restaurant guide

CON TEN TS

TOMATO AND CRAB
MILLEFEUILLE

08

CREAM OF SEA
URCHIN AND FENNEL

16

SKIN-ON SALMON
MI-CUIT IN OLIVE OIL

50

CRISPY
TRUFFLE TART
WITH ONION CONFIT
AND SMOKED BACON

58

LANGOUSTINE
AND TRUFFLE RAVIOLI

24

CAVIAR JELLY
WITH CAULIFLOWER CREAM

34

TURBAN
OF LANGOUSTINE IN SPAGHETTI

42

MACARONI GRATIN
WITH TRUFFLES, CELERY, AND FOIE GRAS

66

LAMB, EGGPLANT,
ZUCCHINI, AND TOMATO PIE

76

SAVARIN
WITH KIRSCH

86

TOMATO AND CRAB
MILLEFEUILLE

Summer's candy apple, seductive, juicy, and with yielding flesh, I love the tomato. It plays an important part in my cuisine because few vegetables lend themselves to such diverse use. Its tart, sourish, slightly acidic, and sweet flavor combines wonderfully with shellfish. This very light, fresh, and colorful appetizer packs a punch with the sweet-and-sour flavors of crab, tomato, apple, avocado, watercress . . . and with a presentation that gives the impression of being part cake. Don't be put off by the apparent complexity of this recipe: It's simpler than it looks. The only really tricky step consists of cutting the tomato flesh into long and wide strips.

RECEIPE

SERVES 4 – Preparation time: 1 hour – Resting time: 2 hours

DRINK PAIRING
Passion Blanche, a Pays des Côtes Catalanes wine from Domaine Bernard Magrez

- ❒ 16 large tomatoes
- ❒ 2 brown crabs (2 pounds 3 ounces/1 kg each), cooked
- ❒ 1 sprig tarragon
- ❒ 1 pinch curry powder
- ❒ ¼ cup (55 g) mayonnaise (see p. 98)
- ❒ Juice of 1 lemon
- ❒ 10 large lettuce leaves

- ❒ ½ bunch watercress
- ❒ 1 Granny Smith apple
- ❒ 1 avocado
- ❒ ⅔ cup (150 ml) vinaigrette (see p. 98)
- ❒ 6½ tablespoons (100 ml) olive oil
- ❒ 6½ tablespoons (100 ml) sherry vinegar

- ❒ 1 dash chlorophyll
- ❒ 8 sprigs chervil
- ❒ Freshly ground pepper
- ❒ Guérande sea salt

TOMATO COULIS

- ❒ 7 ounces (200 g) tomato flesh
- ❒ 2½ tablespoons (40 ml)

tomato paste
- ❒ 3½ tablespoons (55 ml) ketchup
- ❒ 5 tablespoons (75 ml) sherry vinegar
- ❒ A few drops of Tabasco®
- ❒ 5 tablespoons (75 ml) olive oil
- ❒ Celery salt
- ❒ Freshly ground pepper

10

Peel the tomatoes. Cut 4¾-by-2-inch (12-by-5-cm) strips from the outer flesh of the tomatoes. Set aside the remaining flesh for the coulis.

Spread the strips out on a baking sheet, cover with another baking sheet, and let rest for 2 to 3 hours.

Peel the crabs. Use a fork to shred the meat, removing any cartilage. Weigh out 8½ ounces (240 g) of crabmeat.

To peel the tomatoes more easily, cut an X across their bottoms, immerse for 10 seconds in boiling water, then in an ice water bath. The skin will come off without any problems.

Collect the crab mustard with a spoon and pass through a drum sieve*, pressing down with the back of a spoon or with a spatula. Chop up the tarragon. Mix the crabmeat with the curry powder, tarragon, 3 tablespoons of mayonnaise, lemon juice, and the crab mustard. Set aside* in the refrigerator.

Wash and dry the lettuce leaves. Roll up and chop with a knife. Wash and dry the watercress. Remove the stems and chop the leaves with a knife. Cut the apple into batons, and then into ¼-inch (5-mm) dice. Halve the avocado, remove the pit, and cut the flesh into ¼-inch (5-mm) dice.

Don't mix the lettuce and watercress together once finely chopped; they will be used separately.*

Tomato coulis

Blend the tomato flesh. Add the tomato paste, ketchup, vinegar, celery salt, pepper, Tabasco®, and olive oil in this order. Press through a fine conical strainer* twice. Check and adjust the seasoning. Refrigerate.

06

Season the lettuce and watercress separately with a little vinaigrette. Mix the diced apple and avocado. Season with a little vinaigrette. Drizzle the tomato strips with a little olive oil and vinegar, and lay one at the bottom of a 4¾-by-2-inch (12-by-5-cm) frame. Season with pepper and fleur de sel. Scatter a little lettuce on top.

07

Remember to collect the unused flesh from the large tomatoes and use it to make the coulis. You need 7 ounces (200 g) tomato flesh without seeds.

Cover with a layer of seasoned crabmeat, place a tomato strip on top, followed by watercress and some of the apple-and-avocado mixture. Layer over with a tomato strip, lettuce, crab, and another tomato strip. Assemble three other identical millefeuilles. Use a fork to drizzle with a few drops of oil and vinegar. Sprinkle with fleur de sel.

Pour tomato coulis into plates. Mix the rest of the mayonnaise with the chlorophyll. Make small green mayonnaise dots over the edge of the coulis. Remove the frames from the millefeuilles and place in the middle of the plates, with a sprig of chervil at each end. Serve cold.

Prepare the plates just before serving. Roll up paper to make a cone, fill with the chlorophyll-colored mayonnaise, and cut off the tip of the cone. Pipe small green dots over the edge the tomato coulis.

CREAM OF SEA
URCHIN AND FENNEL

A dish is only good if the ingredients used to make it are of good quality, cooked with precision, harmoniously combined, and well seasoned. Here is my recipe for lovers of the briny flavor of the sea and the courageous ones who aren't afraid of getting pricked by a sea urchin. It will be well worth the trouble. In addition, this cream is a uniquely delicate and airy combination of star anise, fennel, and sea urchin roe.

RECISE

SERVES 4 – Preparation time: 1½ hours – Cooking time: 1 hour

DRINK PAIRING

A white Pessac-Léognan wine, such as Château Pape Clément

- ❒ 8 large Brittany sea urchins
- ❒ 3 tablespoons plus
  1 teaspoon (50 ml) milk
- ❒ 1 egg
- ❒ 1 teaspoon (5 g) lobster
  coral
- ❒ 1 pinch sugar
- ❒ 4 pinches finely chopped*
  chives

LOBSTER BROTH

- ❒ 9 ounces (255 g) lobster
  carcasses
- ❒ 1¾ ounces (50 g) onion,
  chopped
- ❒ ½ ounce (15 g) fennel,
  chopped
- ❒ ½ ounce (15 g) carrot,
  chopped
- ❒ 1¾ ounces (50 g) shallot,
  chopped
- ❒ 3 tablespoons plus
  1 teaspoon (50 ml) olive oil

- ❒ 1 bouquet garni (see p. 98)
- ❒ 2 cloves garlic, degermed
  and crushed
- ❒ 2 cups (500 ml) fish fumet
  (see p. 98)
- ❒ 1½ teaspoons tomato
  paste
- ❒ Fine salt
- ❒ 1 pinch coarsely ground
  pepper

FENNEL CREAM

- ❒ 3½ ounces (100 g) fennel,
  thinly sliced*

- ❒ 2¾ ounces (75 g) onion,
  thinly sliced*
- ❒ 3 tablespoons (40 g) butter
- ❒ 1¼ cups (300 ml) fish
  fumet (see p. 98)
- ❒ 1 pinch fennel seeds
- ❒ 1 point star anise
- ❒ ⅔ cup (150 ml) light
  cream
- ❒ 2 tablespoons (30 ml)
  lemon juice
- ❒ Fine salt

18

Lobster broth

Sweat* the vegetables in some of the oil with a pinch of salt. Add the bouquet garni and garlic. Cook for 4 minutes without browning*.

01

Brown the lobster carcasses separately in the rest of the oil. Drain, add to the vegetables, stir, then moisten with 2 cups (500 ml) of fish fumet or water.

Add the tomato paste and water. Cook for 30 minutes. Strain*. Reduce to 1 cup (250 ml). Press through a conical strainer*, reduce by half, then strain again.

02

03

When cooking the vegetables with the lobster carcasses (over medium heat), skim regularly to remove all impurities.*

Use scissors to cut open the sea urchins. Gently remove the roe (gonads). Roll in paper towels. Strain* the sea urchin liquid.

Add the lobster broth, milk, egg, lobster coral, and sugar to the sea urchin liquid. Blend. Strain* two or three times.

To cut open the sea urchins, make a hole with the tip of the scissors on one side of the top part, then cut around in a circle. Use a small spoon to gently lift out the roe. Also collect the liquid in a container. It's worth the trouble; but if your hands can't handle it, wear gloves to protect them from getting pricked.

Fennel cream

Sweat* the fennel and onion for 15 minutes over low heat with half of the butter and the salt. Add the fumet, fennel seeds, and star anise.

06

Reduce* by half. Add the cream, bring to a boil for 10 minutes. Preheat the oven to 200°F (90°C). Strain through a conical strainer*. Whisk in the rest of the butter.

07

Don't let the onion change color and keep the heat on low so that the vegetables "sweat," i.e., release their residual water.

Incorporate the lemon juice. Pour the sea urchin cream into 4 cups. Cover with aluminum foil. Place in a bain-marie and cook for 20 minutes in the oven at 200°F (90°C).

When the cream is set, but still wobbly, arrange the sea urchin roe on top. Coat with the fennel cream, sprinkle with chives, and serve.

LANGOUSTINE
AND TRUFFLE RAVIOLI

I've loved this exquisite dish since I started out as a chef restaurateur in December 1981, at Jamin, in Paris. It gives off delicious aromas of truffle and langoustine, land and sea brought together. Cooking the ravioli in court-bouillon preserves the subtle flavor of the langoustine. Despite its name "langoustine" (from *langouste* spiny lobster), it is not a small spiny lobster. Its body resembles more that of a true lobster.

RECIPE

Serves 4 – Preparation time: 50 minutes – Cooking time: 50 minutes – Resting time: 1 hour

DRINK PAIRING
Le Chevalier de Sterimberg, a Hermitage Blanc wine from Maison Paul-Jaboulet Aîné

RAVIOLI DOUGH

- ❑ 7 ounces (200 g) T45 flour
- ❑ 1 ounce (15 g) duck fat
- ❑ Flour for dusting
- ❑ ⅛ ounce (3 g) fine salt

FILLING AND GARNISH

- ❑ 20–30 raw langoustines such as Dublin prawns (about 8 pounds 14 ounces/4 kg)
- ❑ ⅜ ounce (10 g) chopped truffle plus 1 ounce (30 g) whole truffle
- ❑ 3½ ounces (100 g) cabbage leaves
- ❑ 1½ tablespoons (20 g) butter, cut into cubes
- ❑ 1 tablespoon (15 ml) olive oil
- ❑ Kosher salt
- ❑ Fine salt
- ❑ Freshly ground pepper

VEGETABLE BROTH

- ❑ 3½ ounces (100 g) carrots
- ❑ 1¾ ounces (50 g) onion
- ❑ 3½ ounces (100 g) celery
- ❑ 3½ ounces (100 g) button mushroom scraps
- ❑ 1 clove garlic
- ❑ 1 bouquet garni (see p. 98)
- ❑ 1 point star anise
- ❑ ⅜ ounce (10 g) fresh ginger, thinly sliced*

- ❑ 1½ teaspoons (10 g) salt

SAUCE

- ❑ 2⅛ ounces (60 g) foie gras, cooked
- ❑ ¼ cup plus 1 teaspoon (60 g) butter
- ❑ 1 tablespoon plus 2 teaspoons (25 ml) truffle juice

26

Ravioli dough

Mix the flour, salt, and duck fat in a stand mixer, then add 5 tablespoons (75 ml) of boiling water. Mix the dough without beating. Spread the dough out over a floured work surface. Cut into two equal parts. Wrap in aluminum foil. Let rest in the refrigerator for 1 hour.

01

Filling

Peel the langoustines. Devein. Pat the tails dry on a cloth. Season with pepper, then coat with chopped truffle.

02

If you don't have time to make ravioli dough, ready-to-use dough can also be bought from specialty stores. To peel raw langoustines, use a pair of scissors to cut through the shell over their bellies.

Vegetable broth

Thinly slice* the carrot, onion, and celery. Combine in a saucepan with the mushroom scraps*, herbs, and spices. Add 4¼ cups (1 liter) of water. Season with salt. Simmer for 30 minutes. Let rest for 10 minutes away from heat. Strain through a conical strainer*. Reduce* to 2 cups (500 ml) of broth.

03

Roll the dough through a pasta machine* to make a very fine strip 4 inches (10 cm) wide. Place the langoustines along one side of the dough, spacing them evenly, and fold the other side over to cover them.

04

Shape the ravioli by cutting the dough with a 2¾-inch (7-cm) cookie cutter*.

05

Seal the dough by pinching the edges with your fingers, then cut them again using a 2½-inch (6-cm) cookie cutter.
Pinch the edges again and make sure that the ravioli are well sealed. Transfer to a baking sheet lined with plastic wrap and dusted with flour.

06

Don't lay the ravioli on an unlined baking sheet or dish (cover with plastic wrap and dust with flour), because they will stick and tear when lifted off to be cooked.

Brush and peel the whole truffle. Cut into thin slices, then cut into very fine strips.

Sauce

Pass the foie gras through a drum sieve* and mix with the butter. Combine 3 tablespoons plus 1 teaspoon (50 ml) of vegetable broth with the truffle juice and bring to a boil.

Use a bowl scraper to crush the foie gras through the drum sieve.*

Whisk the combined butter and foie gras into the broth a little at a time. Adjust the seasoning, then strain through a conical strainer*. Keep warm.

09

Filling
Cut the cabbage into ⅜-inch (1-cm) strips. Immerse in boiling salted water for 2 minutes. Refresh (shock) and drain. Thicken with the butter. Season with salt.

10

Bring water to a boil in a saucepan with 1 tablespoon of oil. Season with salt. Drop the ravioli into the boiling water, one at a time. Cook for 3 minutes. Drain and lightly pat dry.

Arrange three ravioli in a circle on each plate. Place a small pile of cabbage in the middle. Coat each of the ravioli with a spoon of very hot foie gras butter sauce. Sprinkle each of the ravioli with a pinch of truffle. Serve immediately.

Don't overcook the ravioli; like all fresh pasta, it will become soggy. Measure the cooking time from the moment the water comes back to a boil, and make sure there is plenty of water so that this happens very quickly.

CAVIAR JELLY
WITH CAULIFLOWER CREAM

Caviar is one of the most refined products that exist. Shiny as a jewel, the little translucent roe look like fine pearls. I love caviar for its strong taste, with a little bitterness, a little brine, a hint of sweetness, and, of course, a touch of acidity. My love for this product began when I combined the complexity of caviar with the velvety smoothness of cauliflower cream. It is one of the dishes that brought me fame. The flavors of the cauliflower and caviar are enhanced by the lobster jelly. The complexity of the dish is hidden from view. . . .

RECIPE

Serves 4 – Preparation time: 1½ hours – Cooking time: 4 hours

Drink pairing
Veuve Cliquot champagne

- ❏ 1 pound 2 ounces (500 g) lobster shells
- ❏ ¼ cup plus 2 teaspoons (70 ml) olive oil
- ❏ 1 ounce (30 g) onion
- ❏ 1 ounce (30 g) fennel
- ❏ ¾ ounce (20 g) celery
- ❏ 1 ounce (30 g) carrot
- ❏ 1¾ ounces (50 g) shallot
- ❏ 1 small bouquet garni (see p. 98)
- ❏ 1 tablespoon tomato paste
- ❏ 2¾ ounces (80 g) caviar
- ❏ 1 tablespoon mayonnaise (see p. 98)
- ❏ A few sprigs of chervil
- ❏ Salt
- ❏ Coarsely ground pepper

CALF-FOOT JELLY (MAKES 8½ CUPS/2 LITERS)

- ❏ 2 calf feet, split in half with bones detached
- ❏ 2½ tablespoons kosher salt

CAULIFLOWER CREAM

- ❏ 2½ cups (600 ml) chicken broth (see p. 99)
- ❏ 1 pound 12 ounces (800 g) cauliflower
- ❏ 1 pinch curry powder
- ❏ ¼ cup (30 g) cornstarch
- ❏ 1 egg yolk
- ❏ 6½ tablespoons (100 ml) whipping cream
- ❏ 3 tablespoons plus 1 teaspoon (5 ml) heavy cream

- ❏ Salt
- ❏ Freshly ground pepper

CLARIFICATION

- ❏ 1 large egg white
- ❏ 1 tablespoon coarsely chopped leek
- ❏ 1 tablespoon coarsely chopped carrot
- ❏ 1 tablespoon coarsely chopped celery
- ❏ 2 ice cubes, crushed
- ❏ 1 point star anise

Calf-foot jelly

Combine the calf feet, bones, and 1½ teaspoons of the kosher salt in cold water and bring to a boil. Simmer for 2 minutes, then cool. Transfer to a saucepan with 17 cups (4 liters) of water. Add the remainder of the salt. Let cook at a gentle simmer for 3 hours. Strain through a conical strainer*. Remove the flesh from one-half of a calf foot and cut into small dice. Measure out 5¼ cups (1.25 liters) of the resulting broth.

01

Cauliflower cream

Bring the chicken broth to a boil with the blanched* cauliflower. Add the curry powder. Cover with the lid and cook for 20 minutes. Strain the cauliflower through a fine conical strainer*.

Reduce* the broth to 2 cups (500 ml). Dissolve* the cornstarch in ¼ cup (60 ml) of water. Stir in a ladle of broth with a whisk. Pour the mixture into the boiling broth while stirring with the whisk for 3 minutes.

02

03

To cool the calf feet well, don't think twice about running cold water over them.
Cauliflower is blanched to remove its acrid taste. Immerse the cauliflower in boiling salted water. Let boil for 2 to 3 minutes, then cool under cold running water and drain.

Mix the egg yolk with the whipping cream. Gently pour a ladle of broth into the cream and stir. Pour the cream mixture into the pan while stirring with the whisk. At the first sign of a boil, remove from heat. Blend. Strain through a fine conical strainer*. Adjust the seasoning. Let cool completely. Adjust the consistency by adding heavy cream, if necessary.

Chop* up the lobster shells. Brown over high heat in a pan with 3 tablespoons plus 1 teaspoon (50 ml) of olive oil.

05

Whether incorporating the cornstarch or the egg yolk and cream mixture into the boiling broth, stir gently and constantly with a whisk to prevent lumps from forming or the egg yolk from coagulating.

Dice the onion, fennel, celery, carrot, and shallot. Sweat* the vegetables with the bouquet garni and remaining 1 tablespoon plus 1 teaspoon (20 ml) olive oil in a saucepan over medium heat, without browning. Add them to the chopped lobster shells, with salt and coarsely ground pepper. Mix well, then stir in the tomato paste, 5¼ cups (1.25 liters) calf-foot jelly, and the diced calf foot. Slowly bring to a boil while skimming*. Let simmer for 20 minutes, skimming regularly.

06

Strain this jelly through a conical strainer*. Return to heat and cook until only 2 cups (500 ml) of liquid remains. Let cool, then remove the fat that has floated to the surface.

Clarification

Put the egg white into a terrine with 1 tablespoon of water. Break up with a whisk. Add the vegetables and crushed ice. Bring the jelly to a boil. Pour a ladle of boiling jelly into the egg-white mixture while stirring. Pour the mixture into the jelly while stirring slowly.

07   **08**

While the jelly is reducing, don't forget to skim the surface regularly to remove the impurities that float to the top. Use a skimmer for this.*

Add the star anise. Let cook at a gentle simmer for 30 minutes. Strain* the jelly through a cloth. Let cool. Let set in the refrigerator.

Warm very lightly to soften. Mold ¾ ounces (20 g) of caviar inside each of 4 consommé bowls. Pour 6½ tablespoons (100 ml) of syrupy jelly into each bowl. Let set in the refrigerator. Pour 3 tablespoons plus 1 teaspoon (50 ml) of cauliflower cream over the jelly. Decorate the edge of the cream with green mayonnaise (made by adding chlorophyll) dots. Add a sprig of chervil.

When you have added the clarification ingredients, let the jelly cook at a very gentle simmer until clear. Moisten a thin cloth (cheesecloth), squeeze out as much water as possible, then line a strainer resting over a large bowl.

TURBAN
OF LANGOUSTINE
IN SPAGHETTI

The fine and fragile flesh of a langoustine easily loses its flavor if poorly handled. It deserves to be treated with every respect. Made at home, this dish has all the flavor, elegance, and delicacy of the restaurant version. It is a creation that is sure to thrill, even at the idea of savoring its richness and purity. Once you have mastered the skill of lining the molds, the rest is child's play.

RECfipe

SERVES **4** – **Preparation time: 40 minutes** – **Cooking time: 15 minutes**

DRINK PAIRING

A Riesling from Alsace or a white Bellet wine from the hills above Nice

- 19 raw langoustines, such as Dublin prawns
- 24 long strands spaghetti
- 3 tablespoons plus 1 teaspoon (50 ml) olive oil
- ⅜ ounce (10 g) chopped truffle + ¾ ounce (20 g) whole truffle
- 1 tablespoon crème fraîche
- 6 tablespoons (90 g) butter

- Kosher salt
- Fine salt
- Freshly ground pepper

SAUCE

- 1 ounce (30 g) onion
- ¾ ounce (20 g) celery
- ¾ ounce (20 g) shallot
- 1½ ounces (40 g) fennel
- 6¼ tablespoons (100 ml)

- 1 bouquet garni (see p. 98)
- ¾ cup plus 4 teaspoons (200 ml) cream
- 2 tablespoons (30 g) butter
- ½ lemon
- Fine salt
- 1 pinch coarsely ground pepper

Cook the spaghetti for 5 minutes in boiling salted water with added oil. Remove from heat and let swell for 1 minute. Cool and drain.

01

Peel the langoustines. Trim both ends so that they are all the same length. Set aside the heads and claws. Make a small incision in the tails to prevent them from shrinking. Lay 16 on a baking sheet, season, and sprinkle with chopped truffle.

02

Once the spaghetti has been drained, cover with plastic wrap to prevent it from drying out. Don't add any oil, otherwise the turbans will be impossible to assemble.

Blend the remaining three langoustines with the scraps*. Season, then incorporate the crème fraîche a little at a time. Pass the resulting mousse through a fine drum sieve*.

Use a pastry brush to grease four 3⅛-inch (8-cm)-diameter savarin molds generously with butter. Line the inside with spaghetti strands. Put in the refrigerator and let the butter, which serves as a glue, harden for 15 to 30 minutes.

Use a brush to spread a very thin layer of langoustine mousse over the spaghetti strands. Fill the space inside with the langoustine tails. Cover the molds with 3⅛-inch (8-cm)-diameter disks cut out of parchment paper greased with butter.

Be very generous with the butter; it will hold the spaghetti strands in place and make unmolding easy after cooking.

Sauce

Thinly slice* the onion, celery, shallot, and fennel. Sweat* the vegetables for 3 minutes in 2 tablespoons (30 ml) of oil. Season with salt. Add the bouquet garni.

06

Sear the langoustine heads and claws separately with the remaining 4½ tablespoons (70 ml) of the oil. Add them to the vegetables, pour in the cream, and season with salt and coarsely ground pepper. Simmer for 15 minutes and remove from heat. Let rest for 10 minutes. Strain through a conical strainer*. Reduce* to a creamy consistency. Blend with the butter and a few drops of lemon juice.

07

Don't forget to check the seasoning of the sauce before adding the butter and lemon juice, and to adjust if necessary.

Place the savarin molds in the steamer insert for a pot. Cover the pot. Cook for 4 minutes.

Remove the parchment paper, unmold each turban on a plate, and pour a good spoonful of sauce around it. Cut the whole truffle into slices and garnish each turban with fine slices. Serve immediately.

SKIN-ON SALMON

MI-CUIT IN OLIVE OIL

Salmon now holds a place of privilege in our restaurants. It would be a shame if the different sources of salmon—wild or farmed—were to make us forget the flavor of the genuine, incomparable Loire salmon I tried at Charles Barrier's restaurant. My meeting with this great, impassioned chef was one of the most significant in my career. The design of this dish owes a lot to him; it all depends on the pan-roasting of the salmon, which leaves the flesh tender inside. This method retains all of the flavor of this quality salmon. I feel it is preferable for salmon to be cooked little, practically undercooked, so that it preserves all of its tenderness.

RECEIPE

Drink pairing

White Bordeaux wine from Château Magrez Fombrauge

- ❏ 9 ounces (250 g) small squid
- ❏ 1 center-cut fillet, 2 pounds 3 ounces (1 kg), taken from a 17-pound-10-ounce (8-kg) salmon, skin on
- ❏ ¼ cup plus 3 tablespoons (105 ml) virgin olive oil
- ❏ 1 ounce (30 g) tomato, peeled and diced

- ❏ 1 ounce (30 g) Niçoise olives, diced
- ❏ 3/16 ounce (5 g) basil
- ❏ ⅛ ounce (4 g) Guérande sea salt
- ❏ Salt
- ❏ Freshly ground pepper

TAPENADE MIXTURE
- ❏ ¼ ounce (8 g) basil leaves
- ❏ ⅛ ounce (3 g) tarragon leaves

- ❏ ⅛ ounce (3 g) dill in sprigs
- ❏ ⅞ ounce (25 g) black olive tapenade
- ❏ 1 tablespoon plus 2 teaspoons (25 ml) virgin olive oil
- ❏ 1/64 ounce (0.5 g) freshly ground pepper

SALAD
- ❏ 3/16 ounce (6 g) dill in sprigs

- ❏ 1/16 ounce (2 g) marjoram leaves
- ❏ 1/16 ounce (2 g) basil leaves
- ❏ ⅛ ounce (3 g) tarragon leaves
- ❏ ¼ ounce (8 g) chervil in sprigs
- ❏ 1/32 ounce (1 g) celery leaves
- ❏ 1/16 ounce (2 g) flat-leaf parsley
- ❏ 4 teaspoons (20 ml) vinaigrette (see p. 98)

Separate the squid heads from their bodies. Remove the beak from each head. Rinse and dry the heads. Reserve the bodies for another use.

01

Tapenade mixture
Wash and dry the herbs. Chop finely. Add the tapenade, pepper, and olive oil and mix carefully. Refrigerate.

02

To separate the head from the body of the squid, hold the squid in your left hand and pull gently on the head with your other hand. Use a wooden toothpick or other aide to remove the beak. Clean the bodies and use them quickly to make another dish.

Preheat the oven to 400°F (200°C). Use a long, thin knife to make four incisions along the side of the salmon, under the skin, placing each about every ¾ inch (2 cm). Fill a pastry bag with the tapenade mixture and fill each incision. Push your finger into each incision to make filling easier.

Season both sides with salt and pepper. Heat 2 tablespoons (30 ml) of oil in a nonstick skillet. Brown* the flesh side for 1 to 2 minutes, then turn over and do the same on the skin side.

Make sure the salmon is well scaled. Use tweezers to remove any remaining scales.
An ideal knife for making the pockets in the salmon is a filleting knife, because it has a long, thin blade.
Attach a round pastry tip with a ¼-inch (5-mm) diameter and pipe the tapenade mixture under the skin.
Use a large skillet with a removable handle for use in the oven.

Transfer the skillet to the oven. Cook for 10 to 11 minutes, then check the core temperature of the fish, which should be 70°F (21°C). Take the salmon out of the oven and let the temperature rise to 97°F (36°C).

05

Sauté the squid heads in 2 tablespoons (30 ml) of olive oil. Drain when crisp. Season with salt and pepper. Finely chop* the basil.

06

Slice the salmon fillet into four portions.

Heat the remaining 3 tablespoons (45 ml) of olive oil with the diced tomato and olives and the basil. Dress the herb salad with vinaigrette. Plate the salad and squid. Place the salmon on the plate. Season with Guérande sea salt and pepper. Add a line of the tomato olive garnish.

CRISPY TRUFFLE
TART WITH ONION CONFIT AND SMOKED BACON

In my opinion, the truffle is the black diamond of French cuisine; it's the product that France is identified with one hundred percent. It's the ingredient that has had the greatest influence on my culinary creations, and which my customers appreciate the most. I love this original dish that I created because of its textures and flavors: a very thin tart crust delicately flavored with bacon and onions, then topped with truffle. This elegant tart is a classic way of celebrating the profound and exquisite flavor of the truffle, the star ingredient of this dish.

RECITE

SERVES 4 – Preparation time: 30 minutes – Cooking time: 15 minutes

DRINK PAIRING
The exceptional Condrieu by Maison Paul-Jaboulet Aîné

- ❐ 4 large whole black truffles
- ❐ 2 cloves garlic
- ❐ 2¾ ounces (80 g) goose fat, very white
- ❐ 3 sheets filo pastry
- ❐ 3 tablespoons (50 g) butter, softened
- ❐ 14 ounces (400 g) pearl onions or spring onions
- ❐ 2½ ounces (70 g) smoked side bacon
- ❐ 1 tablespoon crème fraîche
- ❐ 2 teaspoons (10 ml) vintage Madeira
- ❐ Fleur de sel
- ❐ Salt
- ❐ Freshly ground pepper

Brush the truffles. Peel. Cut into 84 slices, each ¹⁄₁₆ inch (1 mm) thick. Spread out over plates. Trim the slices using a 1¼-inch (3-cm)-diameter cookie cutter*. Finely chop the scraps*. Peel and halve one garlic clove.

01

Cut out 5-inch (13 cm)-diameter disks in parchment paper and rub eight of them with the cut garlic. Grease with a little goose fat. Do the same with the truffle slices, on both sides. Place one paper disk over one round 5½-inch (14-cm)-diameter stainless steel baking sheet, then arrange 21 truffle slices over the disk to form a rosette. Repeat the operation using three more baking sheets. Cover each one with a paper disk and another baking sheet. Set aside* in the refrigerator for at least 3 hours.

02

Place a truffle slice in the middle. Make a ring of seven slices around it in a clockwise direction and overlapping slightly. Then make another ring next to it, in a counterclockwise direction using 13 truffle slices.

Preheat the oven to 400°F (200°C). Spread a sheet of filo pastry over the work surface and coat with a fine layer of butter. Cover with a second sheet of filo and also coat with butter. Place a third sheet of filo on top.

Use a cookie cutter or a baking sheet and a paring knife* to cut out four 5-inch (13-cm)-diameter disks. Place the pastry disks on a large baking sheet, on parchment paper disks. Cover each one with another paper disk and press another baking sheet on top.

Remember that filo pastry dries out very quickly in contact with air. So don't take any sheets out of their wrapper until it is time to use them. Carefully wrap any sheets you aren't going to use and store them in the vegetable crisper drawer of the refrigerator.

Bake for 8 to 10 minutes. Take the pastry out of the oven when golden. Remove the baking sheets and paper.

Peel and thinly slice* the onions. Cook without browning in the rest of the goose fat with one chopped garlic clove.

Chop up the bacon and add to the onions. Season with salt and pepper. Cook for 10 minutes over low heat. Add the truffle scraps*, followed by the crème fraîche. After 2 minutes, add the Madeira. Keep warm.

Cook the onions while the filo pastry disks are baking.
When adding the chopped truffle scraps, heat very gently to release their aroma*
before adding the crème fraîche. Adjust the seasoning after adding the Madeira.

Cover the pastry disks with the onion-and-bacon mixture (use a stainless steel ring mold, if necessary).

08

Take the truffle disks out of the refrigerator. Carefully remove the top baking sheet and paper. Turn face down over the filled pastry, leaving the other paper disk and baking sheet in place. Place in the oven for a few seconds. Remove the baking sheet and paper disk, then sprinkle each truffle tart with a few grains of fleur de sel. Transfer the tarts to warm plates and season with a pinch of freshly ground pepper. Serve immediately.

09

MACARONI GRATIN
WITH TRUFFLES, CELERY, AND FOIE GRAS

Truffle and foie gras in the same dish bring together two star products of French cuisine that are typical of the festive season. I discovered the truffle at the age of eighteen, when I was an apprentice. When I began experimenting with truffles, everybody was familiar with its aroma, but very few people understood its texture. Now the crunchy texture of this surprising product is what matters.

RECIPE

Serves 4 – Preparation time: 50 minutes – Cooking time: 40 minutes

Drink pairing
A great Saint-Émilion Grand Cru Classé such as Château Fombrauge

- ❒ 24 long macaroni noodles
- ❒ 1 cup (250 ml) milk
- ❒ 1 tablespoon (15 ml) peanut oil
- ❒ 3 cloves garlic, halved and degermed
- ❒ 14 tablespoons (200 g) butter, softened

- ❒ 3½ ounces (100 g) shredded Gruyère cheese
- ❒ 2¾ ounces (80 g) celeriac
- ❒ 2¾ ounces (80 g) cooked ham
- ❒ 1½ ounces (40 g) truffle, chopped
- ❒ 5¾ ounces (160 g) truffles, in ⅛-inch (3 mm) slices

- ❒ 2 tablespoons plus 2 teaspoons (40 ml) Madeira
- ❒ 2 tablespoons plus 2 teaspoons (40 ml) chicken broth (see p. 99)
- ❒ 4 teaspoons (20 ml) whipping cream

- ❒ 5¾ ounces (160 g) raw duck foie gras
- ❒ 6½ tablespoons (100 ml) chicken jus (see p. 99)
- ❒ Kosher salt
- ❒ Fine salt
- ❒ Freshly ground pepper

68

Boil water with the milk, oil, garlic, and kosher salt. Cook the macaroni for 10 minutes. Remove from heat and let swell for 2 minutes. Drain and cool.

01

Arrange the macaroni into tightly packed rows over a baking sheet. Trim the ends to make them the same size.

02

Grease eight 5-inch (13-cm) parchment paper disks with butter, then place them over eight 5½- to 6-inch (14- to15-cm)-diameter stainless steel round baking sheets. Use a 4¼-inch (11-cm)-diameter cookie cutter* to cut out eight macaroni disks. Coat with butter and sprinkle with 2⅛ ounces (60 g) of shredded Gruyère cheese. Season with salt and pepper. Using butter, grease four ring molds 4¼ inches (11 cm) in diameter by 1⅜ inches (3.5 cm) in height. Place them over four macaroni disks. Put the eight disks the refrigerator to harden the butter.

03

Cut the celeriac into 1/16-inch (2-mm) dice. Immerse in boiling salted water for 2 minutes, then drain and refresh (shock). Cut the ham into 1/16-inch (2-mm) dice. Heat 1 tablespoon of butter until frothy in a deep skillet*. Add the celeriac and ham, followed by the chopped truffle. Mix and season with salt and pepper.

Use another deep skillet* to heat 1 tablespoon of butter until frothy, then add the sliced truffle. Cover with a lid. Cook for 2 to 3 minutes over low heat, stirring from time to time. Add the Madeira. Cook gently for 2 to 3 minutes. Add the broth and cream. Cover with the lid and cook for 4 minutes.

05

Strain* the truffles over the celeriac. Reduce* the stew until the diced ingredients are coated in the sauce. Season with salt and pepper. Set aside the truffle slices in 3 tablespoons of sauce to keep them from drying out.

06

To slice truffles evenly to the desired thickness, there is nothing like a mandoline.

Cut the foie gras into ⅛-inch (3-mm) dice. Incorporate into the celeriac stew, while mixing with a spatula to thicken* well.

Preheat the oven to 300°F (150°C). Take the macaroni disks out of the refrigerator. Fill the ring molds with the stewed celeriac and foie gras. Drain the truffle slices. Arrange them evenly over the stew.

Turn the remaining four macaroni disks over onto the truffles, with the Gruyère side over the truffles. Remove the baking sheets covering the disks. Then gently peel off the paper while holding the macaroni disks with your other hand.

09

Sprinkle with the rest of the cheese. Drizzle with a few spoons of truffle sauce. Cover with round metal baking sheets. Bake for 15 minutes.

10

If the ring molds are very full and the baking sheets will touch the cheese, lightly grease the baking sheets with butter to avoid any problems.

Remove the top baking sheets. Return to the hot oven and toast the cheese. Press lightly to drain the fat. Slide onto a plate. Heat the chicken jus. Drizzle a line of jus around the gratins. Remove the ring molds. Serve very hot.

LAMB, EGGPLANT, ZUCCHINI, AND TOMATO PIE

I love this summer recipe, when all of the sun-drenched vegetables are at their peak flavor. The choice of herbs and spices (cumin, curry mix, and fresh thyme) give this dish a colorful Mediterranean touch. For an elegant dinner, serve as small individual pies, but for a simpler meal, bake this dish in a large springform pan. I only really came to know and make use of Provençal cuisine when I opened the Restaurant Joël Robuchon at the magnificent Hôtel Métropole in Monaco.

RECEIPE

DRINK PAIRING

A red wine in which grenache is the dominant variety, as in certain Faugères, Gigondas, or a Châteauneuf du Pape, such as Château Rayas

FOR PRESENTATION

- ❒ 12 small tomatoes
- ❒ 8 medium zucchini
- ❒ 4 eggplants
- ❒ 3 tablespoons (40 g) butter, softened
- ❒ Fresh thyme
- ❒ ¾ ounce (20 g) white bread, crust removed
- ❒ 1 tablespoon chopped flat-leaf parsley
- ❒ 1 clove garlic, peeled and crushed
- ❒ 6½ tablespoons (100 ml) lamb jus (see p. 99)
- ❒ Olive oil
- ❒ Kosher salt

TOMATO CONCASSE

- ❒ 10½ ounces (300 g) tomatoes, finely diced
- ❒ 1¾ ounces (50 g) onion, chopped
- ❒ 3 tablespoons plus 1 teaspoon (50 ml) olive oil

- ❒ 1 small bouquet garni
- ❒ 3½ ounces (100 g) red bell peppers, finely diced
- ❒ ¾ ounce (20 g) basil, chopped
- ❒ Fine salt
- ❒ Freshly ground pepper

FILLING

- ❒ 10½ ounces (300 g) lamb shoulder, deboned, trimmed, nerves and fat removed
- ❒ 2¾ ounces (75 g) lamb fat

- ❒ 1¾ ounces (50 g) zucchini
- ❒ 1¾ ounces (50 g) eggplant
- ❒ 2⅛ ounces (60 g) onion
- ❒ ⅔ cup (150 ml) olive oil
- ❒ 2 tablespoons (30 ml) lamb jus (see p. 99)
- ❒ 1 pinch curry powder
- ❒ 1 pinch ground cumin
- ❒ ½ ounce (15 g) flat-leaf parsley, chopped
- ❒ 1 pinch fresh thyme
- ❒ Fine salt
- ❒ Freshly ground pepper

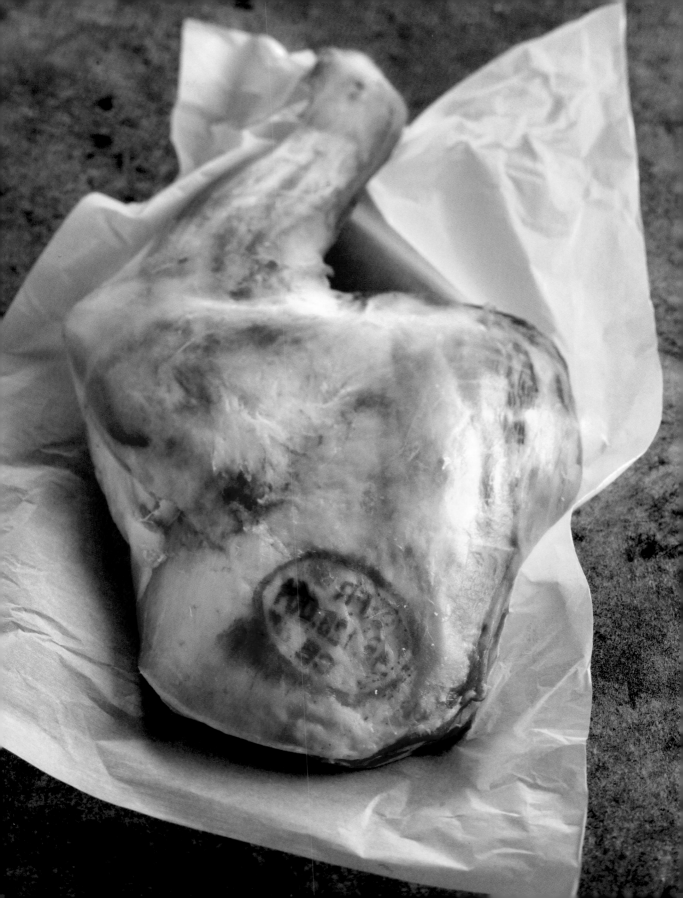

Presentation Quarter the outer flesh of the tomatoes and cut out 60 disks, 1 inch (2.5 cm) in diameter. Slice two zucchini into ¹⁄₁₆-inch (1-mm)-thick rounds. Peel the skin from the eggplants and from six zucchini and cut into 3¼-by-1-inch (8-by-2.5-cm) strips. Immerse the skin strips in boiling salted water for 2 minutes. Refresh (shock) and drain. Grease four 4-inch (10-cm)-diameter ring molds with butter and place on four 5-inch (13-cm)-diameter round metal baking sheets lined with parchment paper. Alternate 12 zucchini strips with 12 eggplant strips to a height of ⅜ to ¾ inch (1 to 2 cm). Refrigerate.

01

Tomato concasse

Soften the onion for 4 minutes in the oil. Add the garlic, bouquet garni, tomato, and bell pepper. Season with salt and pepper. Cook over low heat until the water has evaporated. Remove the garlic and bouquet garni. Add the basil. Set aside*.

02

Peel the tomatoes required for presentation before cutting out disks using a 1-inch (2.5-cm) cookie cutter. Don't discard the inside parts of the vegetables after removing the skin. You can dice or sauté* them, or mix them with other vegetables.

Filling

Cut the meat and fat into small dice. Cut the zucchini and eggplant into ¼-inch (5-mm) dice. Chop the onion.

Sauté* the zucchini and eggplant separately with 1 tablespoon of oil for 5 minutes. Season with salt and pepper. Drain. Sweat* the vegetables for 3 minutes in 1 tablespoon of oil with a little salt. Mix together the lamb, fat, zucchini, eggplant, onion, 2 tablespoons lamb jus, curry powder, and cumin. Add the chopped* parsley and thyme. Season with salt and pepper. Work* the mixture with a spatula until the ingredients are distributed evenly.

TIPS

Partly fill the ring molds with the lamb and vegetable mixture, pressing down well to fill any gaps. Preheat the oven to 375°F (190°C). Fold the ends of the zucchini and eggplant strips over the filling.

Spread the tomato concasse over the top. Press lightly.

Make a persillade: Chop the bread, flat-leaf parsley, and a crushed garlic clove together.

Blend to a very fine powder. Use a bowl scraper to press the persillade through a drum sieve*.

Make a ring of overlapped tomato and zucchini slices (ten of each), then make another smaller ring inside in the opposite direction (six of each). Finish with a tomato slice in the middle.

Press lightly. Season with salt and pepper, and sprinkle with thyme. Drizzle with a little olive oil. Sprinkle persillade over the pies. Bake for about 30 minutes. The top should turn golden.

Tilt the pies to drain off the fat. Slide from the baking sheets onto plates. Remove the ring molds.

Drizzle hot lamb jus around the pies and serve immediately.

Don't forget to gently heat the lamb jus a few minutes before serving. Also warm the plates.

SAVARIN
WITH KIRSCH

Bringing out the essence of a product is often synonymous with seeking out a flavor that is tucked away inside your memories. Cherries take me back to my childhood, when I used to hang them off my ears. They remind me of my first yearnings, my first pleasures. Who hasn't dreamed of at last creating a dessert that manages to draw cries of enthusiasm from customers? Here is one, and it's easier to make than it looks. This dessert is a real burst of flavors and colors. Its jam glaze gives it a very classy finishing touch.

RECENT

SERVES 4 – Preparation time: 50 minutes – Cooking time: 20 minutes – Refrigeration time: about 1 hour

DRINK PAIRING
A Maury or Banyuls wine

- ❏ 1 pound 2 ounces (500 g) cherries
- ❏ Juice of ½ lemon
- ❏ 1½ tablespoons (20 g) sugar
- ❏ 1 teaspoon starch
- ❏ 2 tablespoons yogurt

SYRUP

- ❏ 1 organic lemon

- ❏ 1 organic orange
- ❏ ¾ cup (150 g) sugar
- ❏ 1 vanilla bean
- ❏ 1 stalk lemongrass
- ❏ 1 stick cinnamon
- ❏ 1 point star anise
- ❏ ⅔ cup (150 ml) fresh pineapple juice

KIRSCH ICE CREAM

- ❏ 1 cup (250 ml) milk

- ❏ ¾ ounce (20 g) glucose
- ❏ 6½ tablespoons (80 g) sugar
- ❏ 3 egg yolks
- ❏ ½ cup (125 ml) cream
- ❏ 2 tablespoons (30 ml) kirsch

SAVARIN

- ❏ ⅛ ounce (4 g) compressed fresh yeast
- ❏ 2½ tablespoons (40 ml) warm milk

- ❏ ¾ cup (95 g) all-purpose flour
- ❏ 1 egg
- ❏ 1 teaspoon sugar
- ❏ 2 tablespoons (25 g) beurre noisette
- ❏ 1 ounce (30 g) Morello cherries in brandy
- ❏ A little melted butter
- ❏ 1¾ ounces (50 g) apricot jam or preserves
- ❏ 1 pinch fine salt

Syrup

Wash and dry the lemon. Use a vegetable peeler* to remove the zest. Make sure not to take off any pith. Boil 2 cups (500 ml) of water with the sugar. Add the orange and lemon zests, vanilla bean, lemongrass, cinnamon, and star anise. Cover with a lid and let infuse* for 30 minutes. Add the fresh pineapple juice. Mix.

01

Strain the contents of the saucepan through a conical strainer* to remove the aromatic ingredients.

02

Kirsch ice cream

Boil the milk with the glucose and half of the sugar. Whisk the egg yolks with the remaining sugar. Add the hot milk while stirring. Return to the saucepan and cook until thick enough to coat a spoon*, stirring constantly. Remove from heat and incorporate the cream. Let cool. Add the kirsch. Churn into ice cream in an ice cream maker.

Wash, pat dry, and pit 10 cherries. Set aside* 10 cherries. Put the cherries into a saucepan with half a glass of water and the lemon juice. Add the sugar. Cover with a lid and simmer for 10 minutes over medium heat. Preheat the oven to 355°F (180°C).

04

The cream should not boil (there is no flour or starch to stabilize the eggs). Stir constantly while cooking until the cream coats the spoon; if you run your finger over it and it leaves a clear path, you have succeeded. Before churning the cream, strain it through a conical strainer or a fine strainer to remove any traces of coagulated egg yolk.*

Drain the cherries in a strainer. Measure out 1¼ cups (300 ml) of juice. Dissolve* the starch in a little cold water. Pour the starch into the cherry juice. Bring to a boil. Let cool. Strain through a fine conical strainer*. Set aside in the refrigerator.

05

Savarin

Dissolve* the yeast in the milk. Mix together the flour, egg, sugar, and salt. Pour in the milk. Stir briskly for 2 or 3 minutes. Add the beurre or noisette and mix for another 2 minutes.

06

*The beurre noisette (butter melted over low heat until it turns the color of a hazelnut or **noisette**) should be cold when incorporated into the dough.*

Cut the Morello cherries into little pieces and incorporate them into the dough.

Grease four savarin molds with butter. Divide the dough among the molds, without them filling completely. Let the dough double in size, about 1 hour.

Don't fill the molds completely so that the dough can rise without spilling over. Let stand at room temperature so that the yeast can take effect. The time required depends on the temperature.

Bake for about 8 minutes. Unmold as soon as the savarins come out of the oven.

09

Warm the syrup. Dip the savarins in the syrup until they are well soaked, like sponges. Use a skimmer* to take them out.

10

Pour cherry coulis into plates. Pipe small yogurt balls and join them up with a line made by using a toothpick.

Melt the apricot jam. Brush the savarins with this glaze. Place on plates. Halve the cherries previously set aside. Warm the cherry halves in a little cherry coulis. Place five on each plate. Use a pastry bag fitted with a fluted tip to pipe ice cream into the hole on the savarins. Serve.

GLOSSARY

GLOS SARY

BLANCH

To immerse food briefly in salted boiling water before plunging it into cold water and draining. Depending on the food, this makes it more digestible, removes bitterness or excess salt, makes peeling easier, firms up the flesh, or sets the color. In pastry making, blanch means to whisk egg yolks and sugar together briskly until thick and pale.

BROWN

To cook food until the surface caramelizes; to color a food in a very hot fat or oil over high heat.

CHOP

To cut a product into small pieces without need for a particular size or uniformity.

COARSELY GROUND PEPPER

Peppercorns that have been coarsely ground.

COAT A SPOON

A way of cooking certain creamy preparations (such as crème anglaise) very slowly until thick enough "to coat the back of a spoon," as a result of the semi-coagulation of the egg yolks.

CONICAL STRAINER

A metal strainer shaped like a cone (also known as a chinois because it is shaped like a Chinese hat). It strains liquid through a fine metal mesh.

COOKIE CUTTER

A metal utensil that comes in different shapes for cutting a desired design into dough or vegetables.

DEEP (FRENCH) SKILLET

A round pan with high, slightly sloping sides. Used to sauté.

DISSOLVE

Incorporate a solid into a liquid.

DRUM SIEVE

A utensil shaped like a drum and covered with a tight network of wire or synthetic threads, used to sift powders (to remove large particles or lumps, e.g., from flour) or strain thick liquids.

FINE CONICAL STRAINER

A metal strainer shaped like a cone with an even finer mesh than that of a typical conical strainer.

FINELY CHOP

To cut up food very finely into small cubes, or to cut herbs, onion, shallot, etc., finely with a knife.

INFUSE

To macerate an aromatic ingredient in a hot liquid in a closed pan in order to aromatize.

PARING KNIFE

A widely used, small kitchen knife with a pointed blade, mainly used to peel fruits and vegetables.

PASTA MACHINE

A machine that rolls out pasta very finely.

REDUCE

To cook without a lid for the purpose of reducing the volume of a cooking liquid, so that the flavors are concentrated.

S

SAUTÉ
To cook food in a fat or oil over high heat without a lid and without liquid, while moving the ingredient to prevent it from sticking.

SCRAPS
Parts remaining after trimming meat (excess fat, nerves, etc.), a fish (bones, head, etc.), or a vegetable (skin). Scraps can often be used to make a sauce.

SEAR
To start cooking an ingredient over high heat.

SET ASIDE
To keep ingredients or preparations to one side for later use.

SKIM
To remove the froth that appears on the surface of a liquid being cooked, using a skimmer.

SKIMMER
Large flat spoon with holes, used to remove the scum or lift out food from its cooking liquid.

STRAIN
To pass a liquid through a strainer to remove any solids or impurities.

SWEAT
The action of subjecting food to gentle heat, in fat or oil, in order to remove part of its water content.

T

THICKEN
To add creaminess and consistency to a sauce or gravy.

THINLY SLICE
To cut thin slices, rounds, or slivers with a knife or mandoline.

V

VEGETABLE PEELER
A utensil used to peel fruits and vegetables, thereby minimizing the thickness of the peelings.

W

WORK
To briskly mix several ingredients of a pasty or liquid preparation to incorporate them or make the preparation smooth and even.

BASIC RECIPES

MAYONNAISE

- ❐ 1 egg yolk
- ❐ 1 teaspoon mustard
- ❐ A few drops of vinegar
- ❐ 1 cup (250 ml) grapeseed oil
- ❐ 1 pinch salt
- ❐ 1 pinch white pepper

In a bowl, combine the egg yolk, mustard, salt, pepper, and vinegar. Whisk by hand or with an electric mixer, tilting the bowl slightly for better beating. Add the first half of the oil, a drop at a time at first, then as a thin stream. Continue to beat. When the mayonnaise begins to form, whisk in the rest of the oil in a thin stream.

BOUQUET GARNI

- ❐ A few leek leaves
- ❐ 1 bay leaf
- ❐ A few sprigs thyme
- ❐ A few parsley stems

Over a leek leaf, lay the bay leaf, thyme, and parsley. Wrap with the other leek leaves, then tie with kitchen twine along the length of the bouquet garni.

FISH FUMET

- ❐ 2 pounds 3 ounces (1 kg) fish bones and heads (preferably sole or turbot)
- ❐ 1 onion
- ❐ 1 shallot
- ❐ 3½ ounces (100 g) button mushrooms
- ❐ 1 ounce (30 g) butter
- ❐ 6½ tablespoons (100 ml) dry white wine
- ❐ 1 bouquet garni (see previous)

Have your fish dealer prepare the heads and bones. Peel the onion and shallot. Finely slice together with the mushrooms. Melt the butter in a saucepan over low heat. Add the onion, shallot, and mushrooms. Cook for 3 minutes without browning. Add the well-drained fish bones and heads, and brown for 3 to 4 minutes. Pour in the white wine and 6½ cups (1.5 liters) of cold water. Add the bouquet garni. When the liquid comes to a simmer, let cook for no more than 20 minutes, skimming regularly. Make sure the liquid stays at a simmer. Let cool for 30 minutes so that any impurities sink to the bottom of the pan. Strain the fumet through a fine strainer lined with paper towels.

VINAIGRETTE

- ❐ 1 tablespoon (15 ml) wine vinegar
- ❐ 3 tablespoons (45 ml) peanut oil or olive oil
- ❐ 1 pinch salt
- ❐ White pepper

Use a fork to beat the vinegar together with the salt. Add freshly ground pepper (two twists of the pepper mill) and the oil, then beat again.

BLACK OLIVE TAPENADE

- ❐ 7 ounces (200 g) pitted black ripe olives
- ❐ 1 clove garlic
- ❐ 10 desalted anchovy fillets
- ❐ 1 tablespoon capers
- ❐ 3 tablespoons (45 ml) olive oil

Peel the garlic clove, cut in half, and remove the green core (degerm). Blend with the olives, anchovies, capers, and olive oil. Serve with toasted baguette slices.
To store, add a little olive oil to the container to form a protective layer over the tapenade.

CHICKEN BROTH

- ❐ 2 pounds 3 ounces (1 kg) chopped chicken bones and scraps
- ❐ 1 carrot
- ❐ 1 onion, studded with a clove
- ❐ 1 medium leek
- ❐ 1 celery stalk
- ❐ 1 clove garlic
- ❐ 1 bouquet garni (see previous page)
- ❐ 1 teaspoon salt

Blanch the chicken bones and scraps. Put into a large saucepan, cover with water, and bring to a boil. Remove the bones and scraps and rinse them under cold water.

Put the bones and scraps in a saucepan with 8½ cups (2 liters) of water with added salt. Bring it to a boil and skim off the foam. Peel all the vegetables and add along with the bouquet garni. Simmer for 2 hours. Strain through a strainer lined with paper towels. This light chicken broth is ideal for sauces, creams, and cream soups, among others. Store in the refrigerator or freeze. This will make about TK cup (TK ml) of chicken broth.

CHICKEN JUS

- ❐ 2 pounds 3 ounces (1 kg) chicken giblets
- ❐ ½ carrot
- ❐ ½ onion
- ❐ 1 bouquet garni (see previous page)
- ❐ 2 cloves garlic, unpeeled
- ❐ Button mushroom scraps (optional)
- ❐ 3 tablespoons plus 1 teaspoon (50 ml) cooking oil
- ❐ 1 pinch salt
- ❐ 1 pinch coarsely ground pepper

Finely chop the giblets. Peel the carrot and onion and cut into ⅛-inch (3- to 4-mm) dice. Make the bouquet garni. If you have button mushroom scraps available, chop coarsely.

Heat oil in a large saucepan over high heat. Add the giblets and brown well on all sides, stirring from time to time.

When the giblets are well browned, add the vegetables and do the same. Moisten with 4¼ cups (1 liter) of water and add the salt.

Bring to a boil while skimming from time to time, but not too often, so that not too much fat is removed. Let cook at a gentle simmer for 1 hour. Season with pepper 10 minutes before it is finished cooking. Let rest for 15 minutes, then strain through a conical strainer. This will make about 1 cup (250 ml) of jus.

LAMB JUS

- ❐ 2 pounds 3 ounces (1 kg) lamb bones and scraps
- ❐ ½ carrot
- ❐ ½ onion
- ❐ 1 bouquet garni (see previous page)
- ❐ 2 cloves garlic, unpeeled
- ❐ Button mushroom scraps (optional)
- ❐ 3 tablespoons plus 1 teaspoon (50 ml) cooking oil
- ❐ 1 pinch salt
- ❐ 1 pinch coarsely ground pepper

Chop up the bones and scraps. Peel the carrot and onion and cut into ⅛-inch (3- to 4-mm) dice. Make the bouquet garni. If you have button mushroom scraps available, chop coarsely.

Heat the oil in a large saucepan over high heat. Add the chopped bones and scraps and brown well on all sides, stirring from time to time.

When the bones and scraps are well browned, add the vegetables and do the same. Moisten with 4¼ cups (1 liter) of water (it should just cover the contents of the pan) and add the salt.

Bring to a boil while skimming from time to time, but not too often, so that not too much fat is removed. Let cook at a gentle simmer for 1 hour. Season with pepper 10 minutes before it is finished cooking.

Let rest for 15 minutes, then strain through a conical strainer. This will make about 1 cup (250 ml) of jus.

ADDRESS BOOK
JOËL ROBUCHON

PARIS

**L'ATELIER DE JOËL ROBUCHON
ÉTOILE**
133, AVENUE DES CHAMPS ELYSÉES,
PARIS

**L'ATELIER DE JOËL ROBUCHON
SAINT-GERMAIN**
5, RUE DE MONTALEMBERT,
PARIS

BORDEAUX

**RESTAURANT JOËL ROBUCHON
LA GRANDE MAISON**
10, RUE LABOTTIÈRE, BORDEAUX

BANGKOK

**L'ATELIER DE JOËL ROBUCHON
BANGKOK**
MAHANAKHON CUBE
96 NARATHIWAS RATCHANAKHARIN RD.,
SILOM, BANGRAK, BANGKOK

HONG KONG

**L'ATELIER DE JOËL ROBUCHON
HONG KONG**
THE LANDMARK
15 QUEEN'S ROAD, CENTRAL,
HONG KONG

LAS VEGAS

**L'ATELIER DE JOËL ROBUCHON
LAS VEGAS**
MGM GRAND HOTEL AND CASINO
3799 LAS VEGAS BOULEVARD SOUTH,
LAS VEGAS

RESTAURANT JOËL ROBUCHON
MGM GRAND HOTEL AND CASINO
3799 LAS VEGAS BOULEVARD SOUTH,
LAS VEGAS

ADDRESS BOOK
JOËL ROBUCHON

LONDON

**L'ATELIER DE JOËL ROBUCHON
LONDON**
13–15 WEST STREET, SOHO, LONDON

MACAO

ROBUCHON AU DÔME
GRAND LISBOA HÔTEL
3/F, LISBOA TOWER
2–4 AVENIDA DE LISBOA,
MACAO

MONACO

RESTAURANT JOËL ROBUCHON
HÔTEL MÉTROPOLE MONTE-CARLO
4, AVENUE DE LA MADONE, MONACO

YOSHI
HÔTEL MÉTROPOLE MONTE-CARLO
4, AVENUE DE LA MADONE, MONACO

SINGAPORE

L'ATELIER DE JOËL ROBUCHON
SINGAPOUR
RESORTS WORLD SENTOSA,
SINGAPORE

RESTAURANT JOËL ROBUCHON
RESORTS WORLD SENTOSA,
SINGAPORE

TAIPEI

L'ATELIER DE JOËL ROBUCHON
TAIPEI
BELLAVITA MALL
110 HSIN YI DISTRICT, TAIPEI TAIWAN

ADDRESS BOOK
JOËL ROBUCHON

TOKYO

L'ATELIER DE JOËL ROBUCHON TOKYO
MORI TOWER
2/F HILLSIDE, ROPPONGI HILLS
ROPPONGI, MINATO-KU, TOKYO

CHATEAU RESTAURANT JOËL ROBUCHON
YEBISU GARDEN PLACE
1–13–1 MITA, MEGURO-KU, TOKYO

LA TABLE DE JOËL ROBUCHON
YEBISU GARDEN PLACE
1–13–1 MITA, MEGURO-KU, TOKYO

COMING SOON

SHANGHAI

**L'ATELIER DE JOËL ROBUCHON
SHANGHAI**
BUND18, SHANGHAI

NEW YORK

**L'ATELIER DE JOËL ROBUCHON
NEW YORK**
BATTERY PARK
250 VESEY STREET, NEW YORK

MIAMI

**L'ATELIER DE JOËL ROBUCHON
MIAMI**
DESIGN DISTRICT, MIAMI

GENEVA

**L'ATELIER DE JOËL ROBUCHON
GENEVA**
37, QUAI WILSON, GENEVA

MONTREAL

**L'ATELIER DE JOËL ROBUCHON
MONTREAL**
CASINO DE MONTREAL
ILE NOTRE-DAME, MONTREAL

PRODUCT INDEX

A

APRICOT JAM 88

AVOCADO 10

B

BACON (SMOKED) 60

BASIL 52, 78

BEURRE NOISETTE 88

BLACK OLIVE TAPENADE 52

BRITTANY SEA URCHINS 18

BROWN CRAB 10

C

CABBAGE 26

CALF FEET 36

CARROT 18, 26, 36

CAULIFLOWER 36

CAVIAR 36

CELERIAC 68

CELERY 26, 36, 44, 52

CHERRY 88

CHERVIL 10, 36, 52

CHICKEN BROTH 36, 68

CHICKEN JUS 68

CHIVE 18

CHLOROPHYLL 10

CINNAMON 88

CREAM 18, 36, 44, 68, 88

CRÈME FRAÎCHE 44, 60

CUMIN (GROUND) 78

CURRY POWDER 10, 36, 78

D

DILL 52

DUCK (FAT) 26

E

EGGPLANT 78

F

FENNEL (SEEDS) 18

FENNEL 18, 36, 44

FILO PASTRY 60

FISH FUMET 18

FLAT-LEAF PARSLEY 52, 78

FOIE GRAS (COOKED) 26

FOIE GRAS (RAW) 68

G

GINGER (FRESH) 26

GOOSE (FAT) 60

GRANNY SMITH APPLE 10

GRUYÈRE CHEESE 68

H

HAM (COOKED) 68

K

KIRSCH 88

L

LAMB (FAT) 78

LAMB (JUS) 78

LAMB (SHOULDER) 78

LANGOUSTINE 26, 44

LEEK 36

LEMON 10, 18, 44, 88

LEMONGRASS 88

LETTUCE 10

LOBSTER 18

LOBSTER (SHELLS) 36

LOBSTER CORAL 18

M

MACARONI 68

MADEIRA 60, 68

MARJORAM 52

MORELLO CHERRIES
   IN BRANDY 88

MUSHROOM 88

N

NIÇOISE OLIVES 52

O

ORANGE 88

P

PINEAPPLE (JUICE) 88

R

RED BELL PEPPER 78

S

SALMON (FILLET) 52

SHERRY VINEGAR 10

SPAGHETTI 44

SQUID 52

STAR ANISE 18, 26, 36, 88

T

TARRAGON 10, 52

TOMATO 10, 52, 78

TOMATO (PASTE) 10, 18, 36

TRUFFLE 26, 44, 60, 68

TRUFFLE (JUICE) 26

V

VANILLA (BEAN) 88

W

WATERCRESS 10

Y

YOGURT 88

Z

ZUCCHINI 78

ACKNOWLEDGMENTS
Joël Robuchon thanks Éric Bouchenoire,
chef and Meilleur Ouvrier de France 2000,
and Antoine Hernandez, collaborator and
sommelier.
www.joel-robuchon.com

You will find the videos for Joël Robuchon's
cult culinary show on the Youtube channel
Bon appétit Bien Sûr:
http://www.youtube.com/bonappetitbiensur

Printed on FSC-certified paper sourced from
sustainably managed forests.

DIRECTOR OF THE COLLECTION
Alain Ducasse

DIRECTOR
Aurore Charoy

EDITOR-IN-CHIEF
Alice Gouget

EDITORIAL ASSISTANT
Claire Dupuy

PHOTOGRAPHY
Rina Nurra and Stéphane de Bourgies (cover)
© Photos Gourmet TV productions

STYLIST
Johan Attali

ART DIRECTOR
Pierre Tachon

GRAPHIC DESIGN
Soins graphiques
Our thanks to Sophie

PHOTO-ENGRAVING
Nord Compo

MARKETING AND COMMUNICATIONS MANAGER
Camille Gonnet
camille.gonnet@alain-ducasse.com

The editor warmly thanks Guy Job and his collaborators,
Philippe Gollino and the brands :
Kenwood – www.kenwoodworld.com/fr
Mauviel – www.mauviel.com

Joan Attali thanks Maison Bernardaud for kindly
providing the tableware for the photographs.

Printed in Asia
ISBN 978-2-84123-792-0
Legal deposit 2nd quarter 2015

© Alain Ducasse Edition 2015
3, avenue Hoche
75008 Paris

COOK
WITH YOUR
FAVORITE
CHEFS

PAUL **BOCUSE** PIERRE **HERMÉ** ALAIN **DUCASSE** ERIC **RIPERT** DANIEL **BOULUD**

ILLUSTRATED **COOKING COURSES** FROM **FINEST CHEFS**

TO HELP YOU PRODUCE THEIR **TOP 10 RECIPES** WITH

PERFECT RESULTS EVERY TIME!

ALAIN DUCASSE
PUBLISHING

www.alain-ducasse.com